SUMMARY
of
THE BOYS IN THE BOAT

A FastReads Summary with Key Takeaways & Analysis

NOTE: The purpose of this FastReads summary is to help you decide if it's worth the time, money and effort reading the original book (if you haven't already). FastReads has pulled out the essence with commentary and critique— but only to help you ascertain the value of the book for yourself. This summary is meant to be a supplement to, and not a replacement for the original book

---

We encourage you to purchase a copy of *The Boys in the Boat* on Amazon.

TABLE OF CONTENTS

EXECUTIVE SUMMARY

The book is about how nine boys from humble beginnings cross paths in the University of Washington rowing crew. They struggle with the sport, with themselves, and with each other but eventually win and learn the battles that are important. The narrative focuses on Joe Rantz, his life, and his quest to find meaning in a world that seems to only give him hardship.

The freshman crew shows an outstanding, yet erratic, performance but their coach Tom Bolles, head coach Al Ulbrickson, and boat builder George Pocock see so much potential in them. The boys struggle to find rhythm until Ulbrickson finds the perfect set of boys who would later on win the 1936 Olympic gold medal in eight-oared rowing.

PROLOGUE

Joe Rantz lies dying from congestive heart failure in his daughter Judy's home. *He was part of a group of nine young boys who were able to win the gold medal in eight-oared rowing at the 1936 Olympics in Germany.* In the process of Rantz's interview with the author, Daniel James Brown, he recalls the start of his rowing career at the University of Washington. Their talk about "the boat" makes Rantz emotional, much to the confusion of the author. "The boat" was an abstract concept to him who didn't understand yet the vastness of this concept for Rantz. It was an experience shared by the nine boys during their time together.

Before Brown was about to leave, Judy gives him Rantz's gold medal. She tells Brown the story of how the gold medal was taken by the squirrel and hidden from plain sight for many years. It was only when they were remodeling the house that they found it in the attic. Brown thinks that the story of the gold medal and the squirrel is a reflection of how Rantz's story got buried away for many years.

Brown tells Rantz that he will write a book about Rantz's experiences with rowing. Before saying good bye, Rantz tells Brown that the story has to be about *the boat*.

Key Takeaways

• Joe Rantz and eight other boys from Washington won the gold medal in eight-oared rowing at the 1936 Olympics.

• Rantz recalls "the boat" with great emotion because it is the experience shared by the nine boys that makes it so important.

PART ONE:
WHAT SEASONS THEY HAVE BEEN THROUGH

CHAPTER ONE

The narrative starts in the fourth year of the **Great Depression**. Jobs are scarce and people are hungry. The new president of the United States is **Franklin Delano Roosevelt**. Meanwhile, in Germany, **Adolf Hitler**, the new leader, wants to rearm Germany despite prohibitions set by an international agreement called the Treaty of Versailles.

The narrative zooms in on Seattle at the campus of the **University of Washington** where students are lounging in groups at the quadrangle. The boys had groups separate from the girls. One can deduce that these students came from well-off families based on their appearance.

Roger Morris and Joe Rantz, two tall young men, make their way quickly across the quadrangle. They are both in the same engineering class and have one goal in mind that day: to pass the try outs for the first freshman shell in the university's rowing team. Once they arrive at the old airplane hangar where the tryouts were being conducted, they see a room full of their competition.

Tom Bolles is the freshman coach of the rowing team. He was a former oarsman for the University of Washington. He took up a history degree and is currently finishing his masters' degree. Because of his scholarly look, sportswriters refer to him as "the professor."

The recruits, including Morris and Rantz, are subjected to various physical examinations that day. Most of the boys in the try outs come from wealthy families while the rest came from more humble beginnings: farm boys, lumberjacks, fishermen, and the like. Bolles notes that the physical strength of these boys is important but also wonders if they have the presence of mind to make good decisions when the need arises. Bolles knows that the wealthy city boys might not have the physical strength to endure the hardships of rowing and that the others may not be able to keep up with the mental strain of the sport.

Al Ulbrickson is the head coach of the university's rowing program. He is "the boss" in all aspects - from his clothes to his stature. He was only thirty years old but commanded respect with his demeanor and appearance. His roots were simple. He came from Mercer Island and studied at Franklin High School. This is where he started rowing since he rowed a small boat to Seattle   every day during his four year stay at Franklin High School. His high school saw his rise to excellence academically. He continued his streak both in the classroom and in the rowing shell at the University of Washington where he was immediately hired as freshman crew coach then later on, head coach. His life was greatly defined by rowing and he was determined to get the best new recruits.

Sportswriters call Ulbrickson "Dour Dane" because of the rarity of getting a good quote from him due to him being stingy with his words. Ulbrickson's roots are a mixture of Danish and Welsh. Even the oarsmen in campus know his nickname but no one dares to say it in front of Ulbrickson. He is very strict with the boys. He does not allow them to curse, smoke, or drink. Even as a man of few words, Ulbrickson manages to consistently stir up great emotion and camaraderie among the oarsmen.

Royal Brougham, a sportswriter, tries to get a quote from Ulbrickson about the group of boys who have shown up for tryouts. The only response Ulbrickson gave was, "Pleasing." Brougham is somewhat a local legend with his way of creating engaging sports stories from the likes of sports superstars such as Babe Ruth. Brougham recalls that when he arrived in Seattle, the rowing team of Washington was ill fit for greatness. He was able to see the rapid advancement of the program to what it was now but it was still far from the greatness of being a "world-class rowing team."

Starting from the 1920s, a *rivalry* in bloomed between the **University of California at Berkeley** and the University of Washington. Washington's rivals from the West Coast have already won two Olympic gold medals in rowing. Brougham thinks that fame is about to set its eyes on Washington or even California if either do exceptionally well in rowing.

Meanwhile, in Berlin, Werner March is overseeing the renovation of the Deutsches Stadium in Germany. Earlier, March, Hitler, and some officials visited the Stadium to assess the situation for the 1936 Olympics to be held in Germany.

Dr. Joseph Goebbels is responsible for changing the mindset of the Aryan race to thinking they are superior than other races and nations. He is the minister of public enlightenment and propaganda. Goebbels is "the most important and influential" of Hitler's close friends. He recently put action to controlling of the German press and prohibited articles written against the Reich. Goebbels also pitched the idea of holding the Olympics in Germany in order to show the world that Germany was "a civilized and modern state, a friendly but powerful nation."

At the site of the Stadium or the *Reichssportfeld*, Hitler tells Goebbels that a much more massive sports complex must be built, hence the renovations.

Back in Seattle, Ulbrickson mulls over the "disastrous" season of 1932 which was an annual competition between Washington and California. Bad weather made winning bleak because the lake was peppered with whitecaps. Because of this, the Washington boat became filled with water as soon as the race started. The boat didn't sink but the distance between the two teams made it the "worst defeat in Washington's history." After this, California beat Washington in various rowing events several more times.

At the start of 1932, things were looking up for Washington since they were able to defeat California in several Regattas. They were even able to beat some of the best teams from the East Coast – Yale, Cornell, and Harvard. It is in this light that Ulbrickson's optimism about his team and his potential new recruits were founded upon. But there was one very big hurdle that Ulbrickson faced: no coach from Washington had ever gotten close to going to the Olympics. He needed to find a team that could beat the best team from California and "keep them beat in an Olympic year." But this is not the end of it. He would also have to groom a team that would beat the best rowing teams in the country. And in the eventuality that they make it to the Olympics, Ulbrickson's team must beat the best rowing teams in the world.

Key Takeaways

• Roger Morris and Joe Rantz, both freshmen at the University of Washington, show up at the rowing tryouts for the first freshman shell.

• Al Ulbrickson is the head coach. His life was defined by rowing and he plans to get the best new recruits for the university's rowing team that could beat their rivals from California and eventually make it to the 1936 Olympics in Germany.

• In Germany, Adolf Hitler has his eyes set on making the world see Germany as a force to be reckoned with. His close friend, Dr. Joseph Goebbels, has been conditioning the collective mindset of Germany to be one in believing that they are a superior race.

• One way that Hitler believes will make Germany great is by making a massive sports stadium for the 1936 Olympics to be held in Germany.

- Ulbrickson is optimistic about the group of boys who showed up for the rowing team try outs.

CHAPTER TWO

Joe Rantz is the second son of Harry Rantz and Nellie Maxwell. Harry Rantz's generation gave light to many inventions such as the car and the motorcycle. Harry wanted to "make his mark on the world," so he and his family moved from Pennsylvania to the lumber town of Spokane, Washington. Once there, Harry opened an automobile manufacturing and repair shop since he was very good at tinkering with cars.

Joe's mother, Nellie, contracted throat cancer and eventually died from this sickness when he was four. After this, Joe was sent to his Aunt Alma. Joe developed scarlet fever at his Aunt Alma's in Pennysylvania.

Joe's father fled to Canada while Fred, his older brother, had to leave Spokane in order to study at college. Joe felt alone in his once happy world that had quickly faded away.

The next year, Joe travelled to where his older brother Fred had found a job and a wife, Thelma LaFollette. She was one of the twin heirs to a wealthy wheat-farming family in Washington. Later on that year, Harry Rantz came back from Canada and went back to Spokane to have a fresh start. He married Thelma's twin sister, Thula, and started a home with her, much to the dismay of her parents.

Normalcy was starting to return in little Joe's life when he rejoined his father and his new wife in their home in Spokane. But this did not last long. In 1922, Thula gave birth to Harry Junior and that next year, to Mike. During this time, the light of inspiration in Harry's eyes grew dim because the world was quickly changing and he was not able to keep up with it. He earned his income from a gold mine in Idaho where he spent most of the week, leaving a lonely Thula at home with three children to take care of.

One night when the whole family was at home, a fire started in their home. The only thing Harry saved was his first wife's grand piano.

Joe's life seemed to be thrown back to the time when he was four and all alone in the world.

"Home, it was beginning to seem, was something you couldn't necessarily count on."

Harry took his family to the mining camp in Idaho where he worked because they had nowhere else to go. It was called Boulder City. Joe would often occupy himself watching his father work or he would go and explore and have fun. On the other hand, Thula looked at her current state of poverty and loneliness with resentment. Thula couldn't stand being in the same house as Joe and after a final straw, she made Harry choose between Joe and her. The next day, ten-year-old Joe moved out of the house.

His father came to an agreement with a schoolteacher to let Joe have lodging in exchange for work.

"If you simply kept your eyes open, it seemed, you might just find something valuable in the most unlikely of places. The trick was to recognize a good thing when you saw it, no matter how odd or worthless it might at first appear, no matter who else might just walk away and leave it behind."

Key Takeaways

• Joe was born to a family of modest means. His mother died when he was young so his father, Harry, remarried. Thula, Harry's new wife, disliked Joe.

• At an early age, Joe was left to fend for himself.

CHAPTER THREE

Rowing is an incredibly laborious sport. It requires whole body strength and is not for the weak. It "takes the same physiological toll as playing two basketball games back-to-back" in a span of six minutes.

Joe Rantz makes his way to the shell house every afternoon for training. Coach Bolles would talk to the boys about topics such as the hardships of rowing and inspirational rowing stories to keep reminding them what they are about to get themselves into.

George Pocock watches the boys and their Coach quietly. He is an Englishman who built racing shells.

Pocock came from a family of boat builders. "But George didn't just build boats; he also learned how to row them, and to row them very well." He and his brother Dick eventually gave informal rowing lessons to the British elite and even to royalty. Pocock realized that these boys talked to him as their inferior and vowed to learn how to speak like them. He was able to do it.

After their father lost his job, George and Dick travelled to Canada to seek greener pastures and to help out their father. They struggled and labored to make ends meet but things got better. They were commissioned by the Vancouver Rowing Club to make racing shells for them for a very good price. Afterwards, they got more and more commissions for their good work.

Hiram Conibear would later on be called "the father of Washington rowing" but he had no expertise in the sport at that time. Conibear heard of the two brothers' skill at boatbuilding and sought them out but they were the ones who found him. George Pocock and **Hiram Conibear** met while Conibear was ineffectively trying to row.

Conibear convinced the two brothers to move to Seattle to make shells for his rowing team. Later on, Coniber would ask George for advice about the boys' rowing and this started the improvement of the University of Washington's rowing team. Conibear died in 1917 after falling from a tree.

Dick Pocock moved to build shells for Yale University while George stayed behind in Seattle. George received many orders for his well-made shells from all around America.

George Pocock would then be later regarded as a very well-versed man in rowing. Pocock proved to be such a valuable asset not only because of his boatbuilding skills but also because he was able to learn "much about the hearts and souls of young men."

After training, the boys would make their way towards the training barge, *Old Nero*.

Roger Morris was the only one from the freshmen boys who knew the slightest thing about rowing. When he was younger, he would row in Manzanita Bay. Now that he practiced with the other boys aboard *Old Nero*, he realized that the freewheeling rowing style he was used to wasn't helping his mastery of the sport. But he wasn't alone in this regard. The other boys also found it difficult to master the ins and outs of rowing. They practiced for three hours every afternoon and labored until their hands "were blistered and bleeding" and their whole body sore.

Joe noticed that many of the privileged boys were dropping out of the rowing team. They wanted to raise their social status by joining the rowing team but failed to account for the fact that rowing wasn't for everyone.

Key Takeaways

• George Pocock came from a family of excellent boat builders from England.

• George and his brother, Dick, moved to Canada. They made a name for themselves by building boats.

• George and Dick met Hiram Conibear. Coniber asks the two of them to build boats for the rowing team of the University of Washington in Seattle.

• The number of boys left in training for a spot in the rowing team dwindled because of the strenuous training they have.

CHAPTER FOUR

By the year 1925, Thula and Harry Rantz had two daughters. Harry was able to put up an auto repair and tire shop on Washington Street which had plenty of foot traffic. He brought his whole family back to Washington so they could all be together. Harry was able to build a farmhouse and he started building a house with the help of Joe.

Joe now studied at Sequim school. **He was well-liked by his peers and he did well academically.** He and his friends took a liking to playing instruments and would play as a band in their home, much to the dismay of Thula.

Things turned sour in the household topped with the economy crashing which led to Harry, Thula, and the kids leaving Joe to fend for himself as they moved away once again. As Joe was starting to feel despair again, he resolved to never again pity himself the way he used to whenever his parents left him. He would "make his own way" to "find the route to happiness." He learned how to fend for himself by whatever means necessary.

Joyce Simdars lived with very strict parents. Her father believed in work above all else and her mother was very religious. Joyce and Joe Rantz met in a school bus and their admired each other.

In 1931, Joe's brother, **Fred**, invited him to stay with his family in Seattle. This was an opportunity for Joe to graduate from Roosevelt High School and even make it to the University of Washington. Living with Fred was easier than Joe expected. School was also a delight for him because he made it to the Dean's Honor Roll and joined the glee club and the gymnastics team. Al Ulbrickson scouted Joe while he was practicing gymnastics and invited him to join the rowing team in the University of Washington.

When he finished his high school studies with honors, he went back to Sequim and got engaged to Joyce.

Key Takeaways

• Harry moved his family back to Washington while Joe is left to fend for himself once again in Sequim.

• Joe finally realizes he can find his own happiness.

• Joe is recruited to try out for the University of Washington's rowing team by Al Ulbrickson.

CHAPTER FIVE

By October of 1933, there were 80 boys left competing for a spot in the two freshman boats. Coach Bolles thought that some of the boys were ready to be moved out of *Old Nero* and into shell barges. He chose a select few including Joe Rantz and Roger Morris.

Roger helped his family out by playing saxophone and clarinet in a swing band and helped in their family business. Joe, on the other hand, struggled to make ends meet once again.

Joyce moved to Seattle to be with Joe and to pursue an academic career. To pay for her tuition and other bills, she worked as a house help for a judge.

On the day that the boys who were chosen for the first freshman boat were announced, Joe Rantz and Roger Morris were part of the chosen few.

That December, Joe and Joyce went back to Sequim for the holidays. Joyce's mother showed Joe a newspaper clipping that said, "Joe Rantz Makes First Crew," and told him that he was "becoming quite the talk of the town."

Key Takeaways

• Only 80 boys remain in the quest for a spot in the first and second freshman shells. Joe Rantz and Roger Morris are chosen to train in a shell barge.

• Roger Morris tries to make ends meet by playing instruments and by helping out in their family business.

• Roger and Joe make it to the first freshman boat. Joe becomes talk of the town in Sequim for this achievement.

PART TWO:
RESILIENCY

CHAPTER SIX

Joe Rantz and the other seventeen boys in the first and second freshman shells are being groomed to compete with other teams from all around the country. The harsh weather was very dismal for the boys. Despite the good start of the boys in Joe's boat, it was replaced by "anxiety, self-doubt, and bickering." Even with this atmosphere, Joe's boat was able to out-row an upperclassman varsity boat and Ulbrickson was very pleased.

Ky Ebright, the coach of the University of California's rowing team, had doubts about his varsity lineup because the freshmen were out-rowing them. Ebright was able to build up the rowing team that he coached very well. This sprung the "vicious and bloody" rivalry between California and Washington rowing teams. This was especially brought about by the angry letters that Ebright would write George Pocock in which he accused Pocock of sending his California team second-rate shells. In reality, it was more of his jealousy of the Washington team for having Pocock's rowing advice.

For some reason, the freshman shell was doing poorly. Joe was wrestling with self-pity in his head again. After some weeks, he was back to his normal determined self and the freshman boat was performing well again.

April 13th was race day between Washington and California in Seattle. Everyone was excited to see how the two teams will perform, including Joyce who had taken the afternoon off from her job to see Joe row. The Washington boys beat their rivals in an astonishing record that was never seen before.

In Berlin, Joseph Goebbels and actress Leni Riefenstahl would argue over Hitler's favor.

Key Takeaways

• The Washington freshman team goes down on a slump but rises back again.

• The rivalry between the rowing teams of Washington and California are worsened by Ky Ebright's threatening letters to George Pocock.

• The Washington freshman team defeated their rivals from California in a much-anticipated race

The upperclass varsity team of Washington beat their counterparts from California "with a new course record." Watching the two teams compete, Joe realized that "you had to master your opponent mentally" as well as physically.

Training sessions after their win found the freshman boys in a slump once again. But as the weather got worse, the more they improved on their rowing. George Pocock noticed this and remarked how well the freshman boat was doing. They prepared for the Intercollegiate Rowing Association's regatta at Poughkeepsie. This regatta contributed greatly to the rise of the sport in America. Usually, the eastern teams won until Stanford joined the competition in 1912. In the next ten years, more schools from the West such as California, Stanford, and Washington, would compete. They won quite a number of IRA regattas over the next few years and by 1934, they were finally considered forces to be reckoned with in a rowing world which regarded the East as the natural winner. This only fanned more fuel to the fire of the East-West rivalry.

That year, many people flocked to see the IRA regatta which Joe and his teammates were to row in. The boys from Washington became the national freshman champions, beating Syracuse for the lead. The whole nation marveled at the "stunning" win of the Washington boys. But for some reason, "it was as if the Washington victory had been held up to the nation as some sort of fluke." In this light, California bagged the national championship that year.

All over the country, many people faced hardship once again.

Key Takeaways

• The freshman shell won national freshman championships at the Intercollegiate Rowing Association's regatta in Poughkeepsie.

• The whole country saw the strength and ability of the Washington boys but still had doubts about them.

• The California team won the national championships and was seen to be the lineup for the 1936 Olympics.

CHAPTER EIGHT

After a trip across the country, Joe Rantz was back at Sequim trying to finish building the house and looking at ways to fund his incoming school year. His friend, **Charlie McDonald**, taught him how to use a froe and mallet.

When the school year in Washington started, the freshman boys were now sophomores who were excited for what was in store for them. Over the summer, most of them had read up on what sportswriters wrote about them. **They were being pitted as the lineup for the 1936 Olympics.** This year, they were now under the helm of Al Ulbrickson. Although Ulbrickson had high hopes for the now sophomore boys, he ranked them lowest in crew standings to keep their heads level.

Joe knew training under Ulbrickson would be a much more difficult task than what he faced the previous year but what was bothering him more were personal matters. He was struggling so much with his finances and he finally learned the truth about his family's whereabouts. They had been in Seattle all along.

Joe and Joyce visited the house where Joe's family was staying in Seattle. Joe had good intentions in going to visit but he was greeted by an ill-mannered Thula who told Joe to stay out of their lives.

George Pocock was determined to build the best racing shell. He experimented with a new type of wood to be used for the shell and traveled far to find the best here is in Vancouver.

Because of the rumors that the sophomore shell will become the varsity shell, tensions were high among the Washington rowing team boys.

In Germany, propaganda was being fueled by separate efforts of Joseph Goebbels and Leni Riefenstahl.

While back in America, Joe becomes discouraged by reports in the newspaper that it was not a guarantee that he would get a good job after university. To add to that, he still has about a $200 debt to pay on his own for his college education.

Key Takeaways

• With the new school year upon them, the freshmen boys are now sophomores. There are rumors that they will be promoted to the varsity shell that year which makes the other boys in the crew uneasy.

• George Pocock finds better wood to use for the "best" racing shell in Vancouver.

PART THREE:
THE PARTS THAT REALLY MATTER

CHAPTER NINE

At the start of January 1935, Al Ulbrickson laid out his plans for the upcoming season for the crew in front of the boys and some reporters. He was out of his usual stoic character because that night he was very emotional with his plan for the crew. It was simple: to make it to the 1936 Olympic games. This fueled the boys' "sullen rivalries" to turn into "outright battles." The junior varsity boys noted Ulbrickson's favor upon the sophomore team with resentment and tried to get them distracted whenever they would race.

Because of the sophomore shell's bad performance, Ulbrickson summoned **George Lund, Chuck Hartman, Roger Morris, Shorty Hunt, and Joe Rantz** into his office. He talked about how they weren't doing as well as they did the previous year because they let their emotions get to them and that ruined their form.

Shorty Hunt and Roger Morris had been good friends since they met despite their personalities being the opposite of each other. Hunt was a good-looking young man who balanced his academic life and his extracurriculars very well. Although he was very sociable, he was very guarded about his personal life.

The boys shaped their game up and Ulbrickson promoted them to the first varsity boat but every time he did this, they would get sloppy and be demoted again. This perplexed Ulbrickson. Then he realized that the problem was that the boys focused too much on themselves as *individuals* instead of as a team.

Joe surprised his father with a visit but it wasn't very fruitful for either of them.

After months of keeping quiet, Ulbrickson finally announced that the sophomore boat was the new first varsity boat. The inconsistencies of the sophomore boat proved it difficult for Ulbrickson to stick to his decision but he wanted to give it a shot first. He also wondered why Ky Ebright was so quiet about his team and what new talent he discovered that he was hiding.

All three teams defeated their rivals from California and the bad blood among the Washington boys dissipated.

Key Takeaways

• Al Ulbrickson told his crew his main plan: to make it to the 1936 Olympic games.

Ulbrickson announced that the sophomore shell will be the first varsity boat.

Ulbrickson realized that the boys were still acting as individuals and not as a team.

The three Washington teams won against California.

CHAPTER TEN

Al Ulbrickson announced that it was not a guarantee that the sophomore boat will be the varsity boat in the national regatta at Poughkeepsie. After many trials, Ulbrickson demoted the sophomore boat to being the junior varsity boat. This was settled by the time they arrived at Poughkeepsie and the sophomores continued to display a very disappointing performance.

John Roosevelt, President Franklin D. Roosevelt's youngest son, came to see the Washington boys in action.

On the day of the regatta, the freshman and the sophomore boats won while the varsity boat lost, making the national championship go to their rivals from California.

Confusing reports about an eastern college offering Tom Bolles a very generous paying coaching job surfaced. In the same manner, rumors of Bolles replacing Ulbrickson as head coach also surfaced. Ulbrickson's response to this was that he will quit first before he is replaced.

Key Takeaways

The sophomore boat got demoted to being the junior varsity boat for the national championship regatta at Poughkeepsie.

The Washington team lost the championship because their varsity boat was defeated by California. However, their freshman and sophomore boats won.

Ulbrickson's job as the head coach is put to the test after his varsity boat's disappointing loss at Poughkeepsie.

CHAPTER ELEVEN

Joe Rantz applied for a job at the dam in Grand Coulee that summer. It was a very dangerous job but he still applied for it since he needed the extra income. He also resolved that he would do his best to make it to the 1936 Olympic games.

Al Ulbrickson was still determined to beat California in a 2,000-meter race, an Olympic feat wherein he was defeated once again.

At the Grand Coulee, Rantz found out that two boys from the crew were also working there that summer. One of them was Johnny White. White grew up in Seattle but he and his family fell victim to the economic crash. White learned how to row from his father but his frame wasn't built for rowing so White labored to increase his muscle size.

The other boy was Chuck Day who didn't seem to belong in Grand Coulee but was there anyway. He grew up in a comfortable home but he decided to work that summer.

Joe, Johnny, and Chuck developed a friendship among themselves. Some nights they would explore Grand Coulee and go to places like B Street or the Grand Coulee Theater.

Key Takeaways

• Joe Rantz found a very laborious and dangerous job at the Grand Coulee to earn extra money.

• Al Ulbrickson's crew gets defeated once again.

• Joe Rantz, Chuck Day, and Johnny White develop an unlikely friendship at the Grand Coulee.

CHAPTER TWELVE

That summer of 1935, the building of the German Reichssportfeld was well under way.

Joyce quit her job at the judge's house and found another job at the Tellwrights. Mrs. Tellwright sponsored Joyce's cooking lessons after Joyce cooked a horrifying duck *a l'orange*.

Meanwhile, Harry and Thula Rantz often left their children at home alone without any food or supervision and this was discovered by Joe and Joyce. Other than that, Thula became famous locally for her violin-playing.

Al Ulbrickson made an official announcement that he and his crew will compete in the 1936 Olympics in Berlin. Ulbrickson talked to George Pocock so Pocock can help "fix" Joe Rantz.

One September morning, Pocock invited Joe up to his work station and started talking to Joe about rowing and also about life.

In Germany, Hitler's Reich continued to oppress Jews by establishing laws that limited the quality of life of Jews and eventually, stripped them of their citizenship. Because of this, some Americans talked about boycotting the upcoming Olympics in Berlin.

Back at the shell house, Joe became friends with Stub McMillin who was part of the crew but also took a part time job as the night-time janitor at the shell house. Some nights, Joe would help Stub out in his work while other nights, he went to visit George Pocock. Pocock asked Joe questions about himself and would slowly "close in on the essence of Joe Rantz."

When the start of the crew training came, Ulbrickson made it clear that he would be experimenting with the composition of the boats until "the ideal mix was found." There were two boats that performed better than the rest but Joe was not included in these two boats.

One day, Fred showed up in the shell house to tell Joe that Thula was dead. Joe went to visit his father and children the next day. Harry Rantz told Joe that he was going to build a house for all of them so that they could all be together.

All over America, many people called for a boycott of the 1936 Berlin Olympics but failed after a vote was cast.

Key Takeaways

• Al Ulbrickson announced that his crew will compete in the 1936 Berlin Olympics and asked George Pocock to help him figure out the mystery behind Joe Rantz.

• Al Ulbrickson changed things that year because he dissolved the notion of having boats composed of boys from the same year. Rather, he mixed and matched the boys until he had the ideal set of rowers.

• Many Americans called for a boycott of the 1936 Berlin Olympics because of Nazi Germany's anti-Semitism.

PART FOUR:
TOUCHING THE DIVINE

CHAPTER THIRTEEN

It was now January of the year 1936. Al Ulbrickson warned his crew to be ready to "take part in Washington's greatest and most grueling crew season." Joe Rantz saw his name in the first varsity boat roster along with Shorty Hunt and Roger Morris. George Pocock helped make the boys realize their points of improvement and significant change started from there.

Bobby Moch was one of the coxswains of the crew. It was ideal for coxswains to be slender and light but also to be decisive and alert. The boat greatly depended on their coxswain and Moch proved that he was reliable.

George Pocock gave some advice to Joe, *"... when you really start trusting those other boys, you will feel a power at work within you that is far beyond anything you've ever imagined. Sometimes, you will feel as if you have rowed right off the planet and are rowing among the stars."*

Al Ulbrickson was slowly starting to see his dream team materialize in the second boat. A member of that second boat was Don Hume, a sophomore with great potential. Later on, Joe Rantz became part of boat number two. By the end of March, Ulbrickson finally promoted the second boat to varsity status after weeks of impressive performance. At that moment, Ulbrickson had his star lineup for Berlin: the varsity boat that Joe was in.

In a regatta held at Lake Washington, the Washington crew won against California.

Key Takeaways

• Al Ulbrickson prepared his crew for his goal of joining the 1936 Olympics by making them work harder than ever before.

• Joe Rantz got promoted to the varsity boat.

• The Washington crew proved its worth at a regatta in Lake Washington.

CHAPTER FOURTEEN

After having a two week break from rowing, the boys were back in training. Al Ulbrickson summoned some boys who were doing poorly academically and reminded them of their academic responsibilities.

The boys were told to prepare for the next few months with the idea of going to the Berlin Olympics. A new strategy was hatched on the way to Poughkeepsie and was ready to be told to Bobby Moch, the coxswain of the varsity boat.

Before the Poughkeepsie regatta, the boys visited President Roosevelt's home in Hyde Park and met Franklin Jr.

At the Poughkeepsie regatta, the freshmen won but "lost Tom Bolles" to Harvard. Washington also won the junior varsity race. The varsity boat started with a very slow start, as planned, but won anyway, making the Washington crew national champions. Afterwards, Ulbrickson openly talked about going to the Olympics with his team.

Key Takeaways

- The Washington crew was told to prepare as if they will be going to the Berlin Olympics.

- Washington won the national championship at Poughkeepsie but that was the last time Tom Bolles would be coaching for them.

- With his team in place, Ulbrickson reminded his team of the Olympic dream.

CHAPTER FIFTEEN

After the regatta at Poughkeepsie, even California's Ky Ebright acknowledged that Joe's boat was "the best crew in America."

The Washington crew now headed to the Olympic trials at Princeton. At the qualifiers, Washington faced The New York Athletic Club and the Princeton crew whom they defeated.

Al Ulbrickson was on edge on the day of the Olympic trials. But still, his team proved true and won the Olympic trial. The next hurdle was getting enough funds to go to Berlin since the American Olympic Committee, the Olympic Rowing Committee, and the University of Washington had no money to contribute to the boys' dreams of going to the Olympic games. With a city-wide effort of the people of Seattle, the boys finally got ready to travel to Berlin by mid-July. The varsity boat quickly became household names because "these young men just might be the greatest collegiate crew of all time."

The crew took up the invitation and started training in New York. Bobby Moch received an important letter from his father saying that their family was Jewish and that his father hid this fact in shame all these years.

The crew finally boarded the *Manhattan* and was well on their way to Berlin.

Key Takeaways

• The Washington crew won the Olympic trials at Princeton and was set to represent America in Berlin.

• The whole city of Seattle pooled their resources to fund the Olympic dreams of the Washington crew.

• Bobby Moch learned that he is Jewish after reading a letter from his father.

CHAPTER SIXTEEN

Germany was preparing for the Olympics by arresting non-Aryan citizens. Meanwhile, Leni Riefenstahl prepared her film crew as they were to cover the 1936 Berlin Olympics.

The Washington boys settled in pretty well in the *Manhattan* and mingled with other American Olympians.

Eleanor Holm was kicked off team USA because she was caught drinking.

They all finally arrived in Germany with a warm welcome. The boys of the Washington crew gained about five or six pounds each and felt unathletic from their stagnant state aboard the ship to Germany. This contributed to their lousy performance while practicing in Berlin. Sometimes, the boys would roam around Berlin and marvel at the new city they were in.

Al Ulbrickson and George Pocock took to studying the teams they were up against. The Germans, Italians, and most especially the British posed a threat to the boys from Washington.

The games begun with an astonishing sight that beheld the athletes, Germany, and the world.

Key Takeaways

• Our lives wouldn't be interesting if we never encountered obstacles no matter how much we deny it, so embrace those obstacles and come out stronger at the end of it.

• You will face one problem after another, but do not ever give up since you're only preparing for other problems.

CHAPTER SEVENTEEN

The Washington crew had six days to go before they raced yet they were still not in shape. This drove Al Ulbrickson to forbid them from going around Berlin until the games finished.

Ulbrickson came into an argument with the German officials because the designated rowing area for the Olympics was hazardous in some areas. To add to Ulbrickson's problems, the British crew had the same strategy as the Washington crew: a slow but steady start and then a momentous finish. To add to things, the streets of Germany were restless and so were the boys. Things escalated to the point where the boys from Washington got offended by the boys from Yugoslavia and a fist fight ensued.

As the race neared, the boys grew more serious and closer to each other. Due to this, they became better at rowing and found their rhythm again.

On the day of the preliminaries, the boys from Washington won against their greatest competitor, Great Britain, with a record-breaking course record. As they were set to compete for the medal round, Ulbrickson found out that the lane assignments took a downturn to their disadvantage. Don Hume was still sick which made the USA team's chances of winning "slim to none" because his crew depended on him heavily.

At the medal round, the British and American teams did not hear the "go" signal and lay still in the water as their competitors rowed ahead.

Key Takeaways

• The boys' biggest rivals at the Olympics were the British who had the same strategy as the boys.

• The boys, after a few weeks of being out of sync and out of shape, finally found their rhythm again.

• The Washington team won the preliminaries but they, along with the British crew, were handicapped in the medal round because they weren't able to hear the "go" signal.

CHAPTER EIGHTEEN

Despite their rough start, the boys found their swing and rowed well. But as the race progressed, Don Hume's appearance didn't look good. He went white and Bobby Moch wasn't sure if he'd make it to the point wherein they needed to sprint.

They struggled especially when they neared the finish line wherein the boys couldn't hear their coxswain, Bobby Moch, give orders. Moch devised a plan to use the wooden knockers to hit the sides of the hull to give orders to the boys. True enough, they were able to row in time with the vibrations which led them to their win.

USA came first, then, Italy, followed by Germany.

The boys from Washington won the Olympic gold medal in their event.

Key Takeaways

• Don Hume was still sick and wasn't able to sprint when Bobby Moch needed him to, causing Moch to reassign Hume's job to Joe Rantz before Hume spanned back to shape.

• The noise of the crowd deafened the rowers so Moch had to devise a way to give orders using the vibrations in the boat.

- The Washington boys got what they wanted: the Olympic gold.

CHAPTER NINETEEN

The boys and their coach celebrated their win. All the boys except Joe Rantz went out the next night to celebrate. Joe spent his time contemplating over their win. He realized that during the race, he abandoned all self-doubt and pushed himself harder than he ever did before but with *trust*.

Key Takeaway

- Joe Rantz realized one thing: that he could finally row without self-doubt and push himself to limits he never knew.

EPILOGUE

Seattle was abuzz over the victory of the boys from their city.

Joe Rantz lived in a new home on Lake Washington. Don Hume was back home trying to make ends meet. Stub McMillin visited New York for some time. Johnny White and Gordy Adam went to visit Johnny's relatives, then went to Detroit. Shorty Hunt was honored in his hometown. Roger Morris, Chuck Day, and Bobby Moch toured Europe first before returning home.

By October, everyone was back. "Bobby Moch had graduated magna cum laude and signed on as an assistant crew coach under Al Ulbrickson. Everyone else was back in the boat."

In the year 1937, Washington did another sweep of the Poughkeepsie regatta. After that, Joe Rantz, Shorty Hunt, and Roger Morris went their separate ways.

Joe married Joyce on the same day they both graduated from college. He then worked at Boeing until he retired.

After the Poughkeepsie regatta, the boys would often see each other at least once a year. They would row occasionally until they were old.

The only survivor of the crew in the 1936 Berlin Olympics was the *Husky Clipper* which is housed in the Conibear Shellhouse in Washington as an inspiration.

Key Takeaway

• The nine boys went their separate ways after the 1937 Poughkeepsie regatta but still saw each other as often as they could.

• The Husky Clipper is the only living survivor of the 1936 Olympic games and serves as an inspiration to rowers up to this day.

If you enjoyed this summary, please leave an honest review on Amazon.com!

If you haven't already, we encourage you to purchase a copy of the original book!

Made in the USA
Monee, IL
08 February 2024

53127872R00020